MW00829881

Theda Bassman

Cecil Calnimptewa

Limited Edition

1482 *of 1500*

April, 1994

Limited Edition

1482 of 1500

April, 1994

Preceding page

This is a set of an Eagle Kachina and The Mud Head Clowns, 24¾" high.

Eagle Kachina, *Kwa Kachina*.
(Bassman page 22, Colton #71, Wright page 87.)

The Mud Head Clown, *Koyemsi*.
(Bassman page 33, Colton #59, Wright page 238.)

First Place at the Indian Market in Santa Fe, New Mexico in 1988.
Private collection.

References noted throughout are:

Bassman, Theda, 1991, *Hopi Kachina Dolls and Their Carvers,* Schiffer Publishing, West Chester

Colton, Harold S., 1959, *Hopi Kachina Dolls with a Key to their Identification,* University of New Mexico Press, Albuquerque.

Wright, Barton, 1973, *Kachinas; A Hopi Artist's Documentary,* Northland Press, Flagstaff.

The page number is given for Kachinas in the Bassman and Wright books, while Colton's identification number is specified.

In the captions, the Hopi names of the Kachinas are italicized.

The Kachina Dolls of

Their Power – Their Splendor

LIMITED EDITION

The Kachina Dolls of

Cecil Calnimptewa

Their Power – Their Splendor

LIMITED EDITION

Theda Bassman

Photography by Gene Balzer

Opposite:

Salako Maiden, *Salako Mana,* 5'7" high.
(Bassman page 95, Colton #118, Wright page 249.)
First Place at Gallup Inter-Tribal Indian Ceremonial in Gallup, New Mexico in 1989.

Collection of Theda and Michael Bassman.

Published by
Treasure Chest Publications, Inc.
P.O. Box 5250
Tucson, AZ 85703-0250

ISBN 0-918080-85-1

Book design by The Service Bureau, Tucson, Arizona

Printed by Walsworth Publishing, Marceline, Missouri

This book is dedicated to my husband, Michael, whose love and support made my writing possible.

Acknowledgments

My thanks to the following people who so graciously permitted their Kachina dolls to be photographed, and for their patience with the disruption of their homes.

Robert Broder
Richard and Martha Burr
Steve and Gloria Cowgill
Les and Pam Jensen
Tom and Nancy Juda
Louise and James Lawrence
Wesley Lingenfelter
Michael and Carolyn McGuire
Ruth and Sid Schultz
Nick Smith
G. M. Sollars
Stiesmeyer Family
Daniel and Christine Wolfus
And to all of the private collectors who wish to remain anonymous.

Additional thanks to the galleries who allowed their Kachina dolls to be photographed.

Garland's Navajo Rugs,
Sedona, Arizona
McGee's Beyond Native Tradition,
Holbrook, Arizona
Tribal Crafts,
San Leandro, California

As always, my gratitude to my husband, Michael, who was constantly on the move, getting dolls to me or taking me where dolls were. His suggestions and the much needed editing were invaluable.

Lastly, I could not have produced such a fine book without the artistry of the photographer, Gene Balzer.

Bear Kachina, White. *Hon Kachina*, 17½" high. (Bassman page 71, Colton #87, Wright page 114.) Courtesy of Tribal Crafts.

Author's Notes

I have known Cecil Calnimptewa for nine years. The first time I saw him was at Indian Market in Santa Fe, New Mexico. I really didn't look at him. I was looking at his dolls. I was dumbfounded at such a display. They were certainly the finest Kachina dolls I had ever seen.

As the years went by, I was witness to a tremendous talent that kept growing until I wondered how his dolls could possibly improve. Each doll showed progress, and the power and detail left me speechless.

I have followed Cecil's life with great interest. I have witnessed the happiness he has with his children and the tragedy when his first wife, Muriel Navasie, a great carver in her own right, died unexpectedly. Happily, his second marriage to Wanda Talayumptewa, started Cecil on a new life.

Through it all, Cecil's talent did not stand still. He continued to grow, not only as a person, but as a great artist. His dreams became reality in his carvings.

This book was written to honor a great artist and my adopted son, Cecil Calnimptewa.

Cicada Kachina, *Mahu*, 18½" high. (Colton #263, Wright page 155.) Collection of Robert Broder.

Great Horned Owl Kachina,
Mongwa, 18½" high.
(Bassman page 17,
Colton #78, Wright page 111.)
Collection of Robert Broder.

Introduction

The Hopi Indians live in twelve villages on arid mesas in Northern Arizona. The Hopi believe that they were the first inhabitants of the earth, and are deeply steeped in their religion and traditions. Their spirits, the Kachinas, come into their villages to perform dances, while making requests to the Gods for rain for their crops and for a better, peaceful world.

From July to February, the Kachinas live in the San Francisco Peaks near Flagstaff, Arizona. During the rest of the year they live in the villages and perform dances. The Kachinas are not only the spirits of the Hopi but also the intermediaries between the Gods and man.

The Kachinas represent the spirits, the dancers represent the Kachinas, and the dolls depict what the Kachinas look like. The masked dancers believe they assume the spirit of the Kachinas when they take on the costume and the dance of the Kachinas. There are 300 to 400 known Kachinas, although occasionally new ones are added and old ones are dropped.

The dolls, which are carved from the root of the cottonwood tree, are religious gifts given to the girls and women by the Kachinas in the dances. The dolls are not idols, nor are they worshipped. They are hung from the rafters of the homes to acquaint young people with the Kachina's appearance so that they can recognize specific Kachinas in the dances.

The dolls which have been made since the 1800s are also sought by non-Indian collectors. In the beginning they were no more than stump figures. Later, carvers added arms and legs, and protuberances such as horns, ears, and snouts. Still later, they were adorned with fur, yarn, leather, bells, beads, and feathers. Different types of feathers were used depending on the kind of Kachina.

Butterfly Kachina Maiden, *Polik Mana* or *Palhik Mana,* 9½" high. (Bassman page 93, Colton #120, Wright page 106.) Collection of Daniel and Christine Wolfus.

In 1975 the United States Government issued a mandate with the Endangered Species and Migratory Bird Act which stated that feathers from any bird, other than domestic fowl, sparrow, starling, or pigeon could not be used in the making of Kachina dolls. Many of the carvers attempted to carve the feathers out of wood. Their first efforts were not very satisfactory. But as they gradually increased their skills, it was not long before the dolls became all-wood carved. The next step was to make the dolls out of one piece of wood rather than to glue on the arms, legs, and bases. With the tools that are available today, such as the band saw, X-acto knife[1], wood burning tool, and the dremel[2], the carvers were able to achieve the realism that the collectors wanted.

To make a Kachina doll, the correct piece of cottonwood root has to be found either in washes, or purchased from suppliers who come to the mesas. Not all carvers make their Kachina dolls exclusively of wood. However, it takes a certain artistry and adroitness to achieve the fineness and realism of the top Kachina doll carvers, albeit they are in the minority. These carvers push realism to the utmost. Collectors are looking for a realism and beauty which faithfully depicts the tradition and creativity of the Kachina in the dances. The one piece, all-wood carved dolls are greatly prized.

One of the most noted of the Kachina doll carvers is Cecil Calnimptewa, Jr. His artistry is exhibited in the fine detail of belts, sashes, and garments as well as the musculature, the motion, and the active stance of the doll. He produces very realistic figures which have sheer aesthetic beauty and display tremendous power.

The strides that Cecil Calnimptewa has made in his art over the past nineteen years are shown in the pages of this book. Nine of his early dolls, made in the 1970s, depict what the best of Kachina doll carving was like at that time. As a result, his early dolls have also become sought-after collectibles. The photographs on pages 46 to 63 demonstrate the differences between his early work and his latest pieces. The contrast is tremendous and one cannot help but have a feeling of awe when looking at what Calnimptewa is creating today. His carving is a fine art.

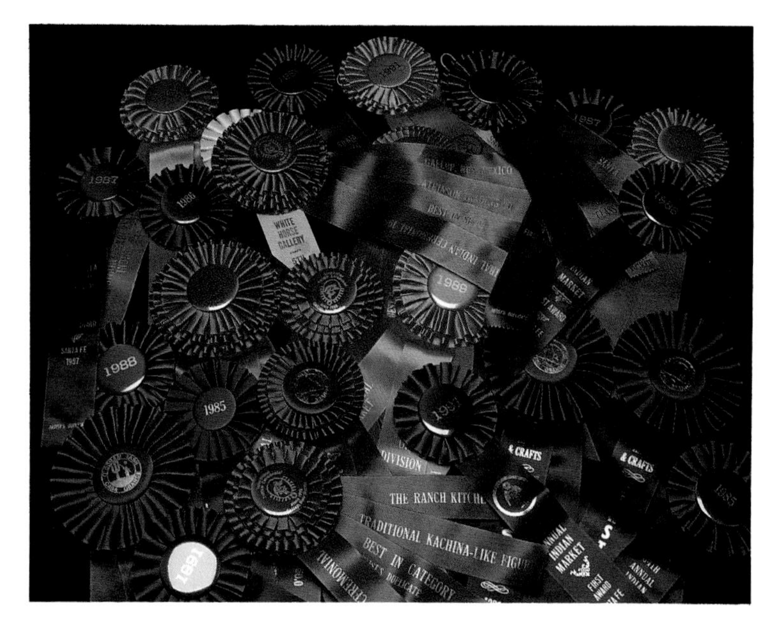

Some of the carvers have become very ingenious in making the all-wood, one piece dolls realistic, but none surpasses the exquisite work of Cecil Calnimptewa, Jr.

---

1 X-acto blade: A very fine sharp-bladed hand tool
2 Dremel: A small electric power tool

Cecil Calnimptewa

Cecil Calnimptewa, Jr., from the village of Moencopi, Arizona, was born on January 1, 1950. He is a member of the Bamboo Clan.

"As soon as I was old enough, I started helping my dad in the fields with the planting of corn, watermelon, peaches, and other crops," said Cecil. "At that time there were no jobs to be had, so my four brothers and two sisters all worked in the fields, too. We grew enough food so that it lasted us through the winter. It was hard work, but it is the Hopi tradition to grow your own food."

Even though Cecil now earns enough to provide food for his family, he still grows some crops with the help of his older daughters, Marissa and Daphne.

Cecil's first wife, Muriel Navasie, also a famous doll carver, passed away on October 19, 1988. Cecil says that he doesn't know how he was able to work and take care of his four children following her death. However, the two older girls helped with the cleaning, cooking and washing.

"Muriel chose the place on Hopi Partition Land where our house was to be and I built a house for her," said Cecil. "The house always belongs to the wife and if she dies it belongs to the youngest daughter. When a boy grows up and gets married, he too builds a house for his wife. The fields belong to the husband so he can provide food for his family. The cars and trucks are owned jointly."

Cecil and Wanda Talayumptewa married in April, 1991. They had originally met in 1971 when both were attending school at Haskell Junior College in Kansas. After leaving school, they went their separate ways. Cecil met Muriel, they married and had four children; Marissa, Daphne, Poeceille-Mana, and Durand. Two years after Muriel passed away, Wanda and Cecil met again. They renewed their friendship, fell in love and were married four months later.

Wanda has two sons from a previous marriage, sixteen year old Dustin and nine year old Jared who live with them. "The boys get along with my children pretty well," Cecil said. "People call us the Brady Bunch. I always wanted to have another son and it feels good. The boys call me 'Dad' and I like that. My daughter Poeceille-Mana and my son Durand call Wanda 'Mom.'

"Now I just have to work hard and Wanda is willing to do that too, as we have six children to take care of. She is looking forward to working in the Calnimptewa Gallery as soon as she completes her bookkeeping and selling training. I opened the gallery in June, 1990 so that I would have something to fall back on when I get old and can't carve anymore."

Left-handed Kachina, *Suy-ang-e-vif,* 14" high. (Bassman page 86, Colton #95, Wright page 32.) Collection of Michael and Carolyn McGuire.

"My father, Cecil, Sr. used to carve dolls and weave all the garments that the Kachinas wear, such as sashes, capes, and wedding robes. Maybe that's why I'm talented. I take after my dad," Cecil said proudly. "I never helped him with his weavings, but I did sand his dolls. When I was eighteen years old, I carved my first doll, the Left-handed Kachina. My dad took it into Zuni, New Mexico and sold it for $50.00 which was a lot of money for that time. From then on my dad and I would carve together until a friend of mine, Tom Holmes and I decided that we would carve down in the kiva[3] because it was always cool there. We only used a pocket knife in those days."

Today, Cecil does not use a pocket knife. He uses a band saw to cut out the figures, then a dremel[2] tool with its various bits to shape the wood. He details the doll with an X-acto blade[1]. "The detail work really slows me down," Cecil said, "especially the kind I do. After I have completed the detail work, I sand certain parts of the doll that have to be smooth, such as the face. But I like to leave the body kind of rough so that the texture of the wood shows."

Cecil feels indebted to Brian Honyouti and Ronald Honyouti and Lowell Talashoma. They were the first of the carvers to use wood stains instead of latex and acrylic paints.

---

[1] X-acto blade: A very fine sharp-bladed hand tool
[2] Dremel: A small electric power tool
[3] Kiva: An underground ceremonial chamber

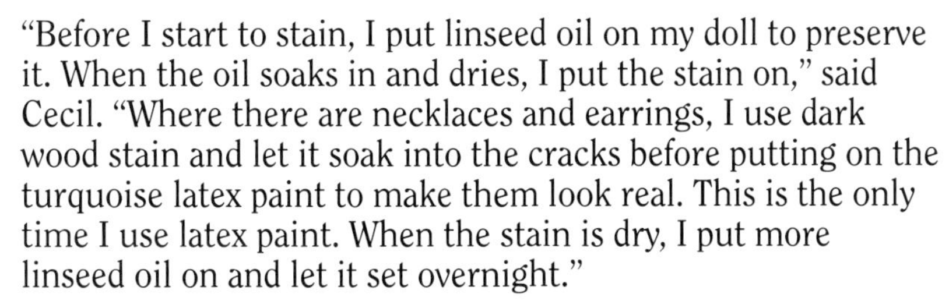

"Before I start to stain, I put linseed oil on my doll to preserve it. When the oil soaks in and dries, I put the stain on," said Cecil. "Where there are necklaces and earrings, I use dark wood stain and let it soak into the cracks before putting on the turquoise latex paint to make them look real. This is the only time I use latex paint. When the stain is dry, I put more linseed oil on and let it set overnight."

Cecil considers a one-piece doll to be one that has the doll, the base, the arms and the legs carved out of one piece of wood. Small pieces, such as bells, shells, and feathers are made separately and then glued on. "If they were carved on the doll, they would be different sizes instead of being the same size. That's why I carve them out of a long piece of wood," he said.

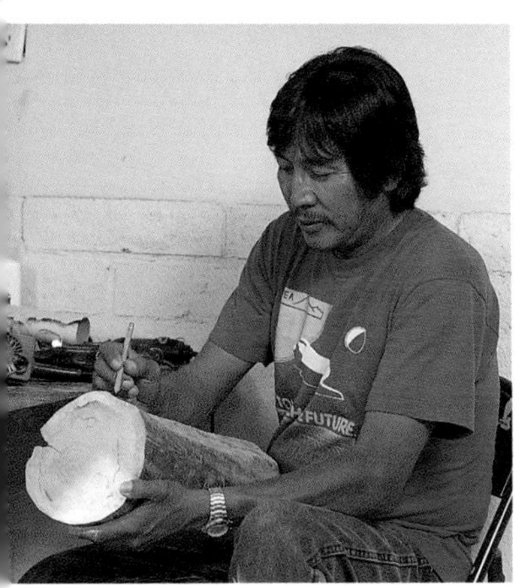

Cecil likes the dolls that are made today rather than those made ten to fifteen years ago. He likes the muscle tone and the action, and also the fact that the feathers and fur are carved out of wood. He gives credit to Alvin James, Brian Honyouti, and Ronald Honyouti for the beginning of the action and one-piece dolls. "The carving of Alvin James had a big influence on me. At the time I started to carve," Cecil said, "Alvin was the top carver and was doing very nice work. Every time I saw his dolls, I admired them. I think he started the more realistic action carving and the nice faces. I tried to push myself to see if I could carve like he did."

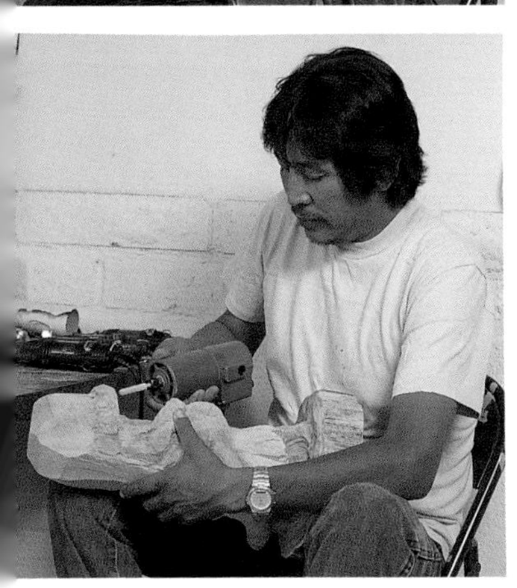

"There are a lot of good carvers out there. I like the work of Loren Phillips, Dennis Tewa, Alvin Navasie, Brian Laban, Brian Honyouti, and Ronald Honyouti, and a lot of young carvers that I don't even know,"Cecil said admiringly.

"I try to make the dolls the way the Kachinas are dressed in the dances. I don't think I would change anything to make them look different. That's very important to me," he continued. "When I was growing up I always participated in the dances, but when I got married and moved from my village it was too hard for me to travel back and forth. I now look forward to being in the dances again with the start of my new life."

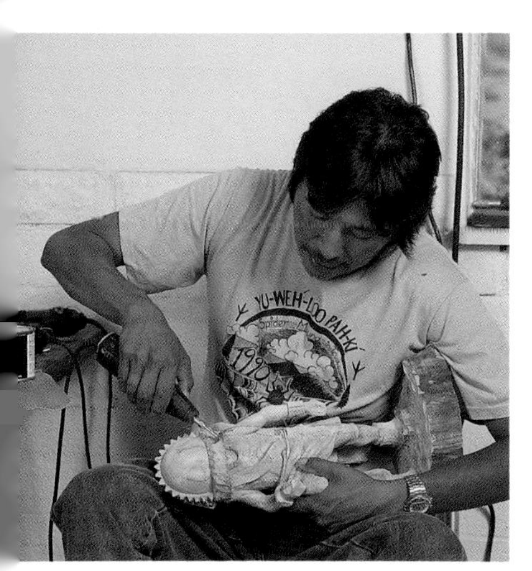

Two years ago Cecil took part in the Heoto Dance in the village of Old Oraibi, and last year he danced in the Corn Dance in Bacavi. He danced with Wanda's son, Dustin. He said that it made him feel good to have Dustin take part in the dance.

Wanda took food down to the kiva for the Kachinas, and when the dance was over she washed the paint from Cecil's body and took his clothes home to wash.

"This is what the women do," said Cecil. "If a man doesn't have a wife, his mother or his sister will do this for him. Women are not supposed to handle the Kachinas, and they can't take part in the Kachina dances. The women can dance in the basket dance, because it is a social dance, not a Kachina dance. If a Kachina drops a bell, a woman can't pick it up and fix it. Only men can do that. Nobody can touch a Kachina for four days except his wife when she washes the paint off his body."

Cecil continued, "Everything in Hopi is four days. After the dance you can't sleep with your wife until after four days because you still have the Kachina spirit in you and it won't come out until four days are up. If someone in the family dies, you can't work on a Kachina doll until after four days because the doll still has its spirit and the person who died has just lost their spirit. The spirit leaves the body and goes up. If you are taking part in a Kachina dance and someone dies in your family, you can't go see him, as the dead person and the Kachina have different spirits and they should not come together."

Cecil said he really enjoys taking part in the dances. It makes him happy and he wants to participate even more. He feels closer to his family, to the Hopi people, and to people all over the world.

"One year after I was initiated into the Kachina Cult, my godfather, Howard Lomatewama, dressed me as a Yellow Fox for the Kachina dance. He was of the Yellow Fox clan. The Yellow Fox is my friend and if I would ever carve that doll, I would never sell it, " said Cecil. "My son, Durand was initiated when he was ten years old and he chose Roger Suetopka to be his godfather. Roger has been around the house a lot and all my kids call him their second dad." Cecil went on, "Durand is now old enough to participate in the ceremonials and to assume more responsibility around the house. He helps in the care of the fields, the animals, and with the planting. The Calnimptewa family grows corn, melons, beans, squash, tomatoes, and chili. We have forty cows and five horses. Durand helps to round them up and to see that the troughs are filled with water every morning and afternoon. When he comes home from school he empties the trash, waters the trees, and helps to keep the yard clean. This winter he will take over the chopping of wood. He helps me a lot."

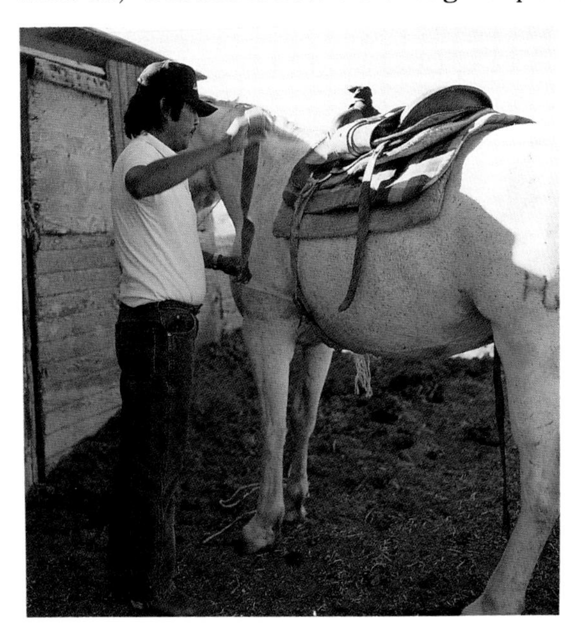

Durand is of the Spider Clan, the clan of his mother, Muriel. When he was initiated he also became a member of the Coyote Clan because this is the clan of his godfather, Roger.

"Last August I sponsored a Butterfly Dance for my three daughters in my village of Moencopi. I wanted to do this because I felt that my oldest daughter Marissa, would not be dancing again. She finished high school and enjoys living in the city rather than in the village. It was a lot of fun," Cecil said laughingly, "but a lot of work, too." Three weeks before the dance, the Calnimptewa family moved their mattresses, bedding, and clothing to the village because they would be practicing every day. They also brought a refrigerator in which to keep the sheep that Cecil's mother and sisters butchered. The sheep was to feed the dancers and the many relatives and people from other villages who came to participate in the dance. Over five hundred people came to the dance. Two dance groups came from the village of Polacca, one from Moencopi, one from Bacavi and another from Old Oraibi. Alice, Cecil's mother, made piki[4], while Lucinda and Beverly, Cecil's sisters, made stew, corn bread, and pies. Many of the relatives made and brought food too. After the dance, Cecil said that although his daughters were tired, they enjoyed the dance so much that they wished they could have danced for another day.

"When the dance was over," said Cecil, "I had to stay in my village for four days as I said before, everything in Hopi is four days. It took me quite a while to get back to carving because I was still filled up with the joy and excitement of the dance."

Cecil's day begins when he feeds his animals first thing in the morning. He considers that the cows, horses, and dogs are his children, too. He also cleans up the yard because he said that the house looks happy if the yard is clean. He runs a few miles and then prays before he begins to carve.

Because Hopi tradition is very important to him, he uses only cottonwood root, never the branches. He said that is just like having rules, and one has to follow them. Tribal elders taught Cecil that the Hopi tradition is never to burn the wood shavings from the dolls because the shavings are a part of the spirit. He puts the shavings in his fields to help the crops grow.

"I feel that the doll is alive and has a soul when I start carving it," Cecil said. "I don't put the eyes on a doll until I am finished painting it. I tell it that I don't want it to see itself until I am almost finished. When I am carving, the dolls don't really talk to me, but I have a feeling that they do. At night I don't leave my unfinished dolls in the carving room which is outside the house.

4 Piki: A type of Hopi bread made from blue corn

I bring them into the house with the rest of the family as they are part of the family and are being brought to life. When I am all finished carving, I say 'Kwakwaï,' thank you."

Cecil feels that he must finish a doll once he has started it. He feels bad to see them sitting around unfinished. He would never throw a doll away since he feels that it is a member of the family. He may give the doll to another carver to finish, one that he is confident would do as good a job as he would.

Cecil likes to help young carvers. A typical day will usually find a group of them carving together at his house. Oriel Navasie, D'Armon Kootswatewa, Brian Laban, Wally Navasie, and Roger Suetopka are his pupils. Dennis Tewa was his first student. Cecil enjoys having the carvers around. He says that the carving and the day goes faster.

"I get excited when I see a doll that a young carver has done," said Cecil. "I say, 'Wow, it's nice!' They do things with their dolls, and I wonder why I never thought of doing it that way."

"We listen to country western music when we carve or sometimes we put on a Kachina tape and hum along with it and chant. I like to sing Kachina songs to myself as I think about what to carve next. If it comes to my mind, I'll put down the doll I am working on and cut out the other doll before I forget what it will look like. That's why I always have five or six dolls sitting around in front of me." He continued, "I always have a spiritual feeling about the doll I am carving. The dolls are a part of me and I am a part of them, too. I talk to them while I am carving and ask for rain, and ask that the crops will be good. I ask them to pray for people, not just for the Hopi but for everyone in the world, and to pray that people would not fight with each other."

"When I sell a doll," he went on, "it makes me feel sad. But I know the doll has to go one way and I have to go another way. I tell the doll that it is going to a nice home and that people will take care of it and talk to it as I do. I tell it to watch over the people, and their house, and to protect them and teach them good things. Then the doll has a happy look on its face."

Cecil tries not to "fall in love" with his dolls because it would be too difficult to sell them. Just like his animals, they are all a part of the family.

Cecil makes about fifteen dolls a year and likes to work on dolls over twelve inches tall. He feels that smaller dolls are too fragile and he doesn't have the patience for them.

The last Kachina dance of the year is the Home Dance, when the Kachinas themselves, not the dolls, prepare to return to their home in the San Francisco Peaks near Flagstaff, Arizona. The Hopi people believe that the Kachinas come out as clouds and rain and go all over the world to help people. At that dance the priest proclaims to the Kachinas, "I am giving you your prayer feathers from my heart and from all the people who are here today. We have all prayed and I tell you this for all of them." So when Cecil met a woman from Germany who owned one of his dolls, he was thrilled that someone from so far away had one of his Kachina dolls to watch over her if she became ill or needed help, and also to help her spiritually.

When Cecil's grandfather was born he was given the Calnimptewa name, which means 'a baby eagle wrapped in a blanket.' As a consequence, Cecil has a special feeling for eagles. Interestingly, at one time eagles used to nest on

the cliff in Old Oraibi very close to the location of the Calnimptewa Gallery. Even though Cecil likes to carve Eagle Kachinas more than any other doll, he also enjoys making animal Kachinas because of their power. Whenever he carves an animal Kachina doll he always says, "Hey, give me more power so I can be powerful like you."

Cecil feels good when he sees his older Kachina dolls. He would like to fix them up and improve them in the style that he carves today. However, he admits that his older dolls seem happy the way they are.

In 1985 Cecil had the Maswik Kachin-mana and Eagle Kachina made into bronzes. He feels that today he could do a better job and would like to do a larger bronze Eagle with more action.

"I like the all-wood carved dolls better than the ones with the fur and feathers," Cecil remarked, "They stay looking good for their whole lives. I like the way I am carving. It is a challenge every time I carve, especially when I am doing a set of two or three figures on the same base. I wonder how it will turn out, but I have faith in myself. When my Deer Family Kachina doll set won Best of Show at the Gallup Inter-Tribal Indian Ceremonial in 1988 it gave me more power to do better work. I felt very good when the book *Hopi Kachina Dolls and Their Carvers* was published in 1991 because it helped the carvers. It was wonderful for me to see the Deer Family on the front cover. I am also very excited about having a book written about me."

"I improved over the years and would still like to improve," Cecil continued. "I always like to challenge myself. With each doll I make I can see little things that I can do better. I find that I am competing against myself, not against the other carvers. I feel that I am starting my life all over again with a new family. Wanda is right there beside me, telling me that I can do it. I also want to keep my traditions as a Hopi to make myself a better person."

Deer Kachinas, *Sowí-ing Kachinas,* entitled, "The Deer Family," 19" high.
(Bassman page 155, Colton #91, Wright page 166.)
Best of Show, Best of Class, Best of Division, and First Place at Gallup Inter-Tribal Indian Ceremonial in Gallup, New Mexico in 1988.

Collection of Tom and Nancy Juda.

Flute Kachina, *Lenang,* 16½" high. (Colton #106, Wright page 36.)
Collection of Tom and Nancy Juda.

Eagle Kachina, *Kwa Kachina*, 20" high.
(Bassman page 22, Colton #71, Wright page 87)
Collection of Theda and Michael Bassman.

Ogre, White, *Wiharu,* 17½" hig
(Bassman page 11, Colton #3
Wright page 8

First Place at Gallup Inter-Tribal Indi
Ceremonial in Gallup, New Mexico in 19

Collection of Tom and Nancy Ju

Cumulus Cloud Kachina, *Tukwünag,* 14¾" high.
(Colton #97, Wright page 246.)
Private collection.

Apache Kachina, *Yoche,* 15½" high.
(Colton #205, Wright page 145.)
Collection of Tom and Nancy Juda.

Green Faced Hu Kachina or Whipper Kachina's Uncle, *Tungwup Ta-amu,* 15" high. (Colton #15, Wright page 24.) Courtesy of Garland's Navajo Rugs.

Snake Dancers, *Chusona,* base is 18" long, 3" high. Snake dancers are 6" high. (Bassman page 8.) Signed by Cecil Calnimptewa and his late wife, Muriel Navasie. Collection of Tom and Nancy Juda.

Broad-faced Kachina, *Wuyak-ku-ita,* 19¾" high.
(Bassman page 23, Colton #22, Wright page 26.)
Best of Category and First Place at Gallup
Inter-Tribal Indian Ceremonial in 1988.
Collection of Theda and Michael Bassman.

Left, Deer Kachina, *Sowí-ing Kachina,* 17¾" high.
(Bassman page 155, Colton #91, Wright page 166.) Private collection.

Middle, Mountain Sheep Kachina, *Pang Kachina,* 20" high.
(Bassman page 121, Colton #92.) Private collection.

Right, Antelope Kachina, *Chöf Kachina,* 20" high.
(Colton #90, Wright page 165.) Private collection.

Opposite:

Left, Butterfly Girl, *Poli Mana,* 16" high.
(Bassman page 84.)
Private collection

Right, Butterfly Kachina Maiden,
Polik Mana or *Palhik Mana,* 16½" high.
(Bassman page 93, Colton #120, Wright page 106.)
Private collection.

A set entitled, "The Mighty Ones."
It consists of an Eagle Kachina and a Red-tailed Hawk Kachina, 17¼" high.

Eagle Kachina, *Kwa Kachin*a.
(Bassman page 22, Colton #71, Wright page 87.)

Red-tailed Hawk Kachina, *Palakwai.*
(Bassman page 112, Colton #73, Wright page 61.)
Best of Division and First Place at the Indian Market in Santa Fe, New Mexico in 1987.
Collection of Tom and Nancy Juda.

A set of an Eagle Kachina and a Wolf Kachina, 21¼" high.

Eagle Kachina, *Kwa Kachina*. (Bassman page 22, Colton #71, Wright page 87.)

Wolf Kachina, *Kweo*. (Bassman page 127, Colton #86, Wright page 164.) Collection of Wesley Lingenfelter.

Zuñi Fire God, *Cholawitze,* 11¾" high. (Bassman page 25, Colton #151, Wright page 128.) Collection of Tom and Nancy Juda.

Left, Navajo Kachina, *Tasaf Kwivi Kachina,* 16¾" high.
(Bassman page 25, Colton #137, Wright page 188.)
Collection of Tom and Nancy Juda.

Right, Proud War God Kachina, *Pö-ökang Kwivi Kachina,* 15" high.
(Bassman page 24, Colton #180, Wright page 138.)
Collection of Tom and Nancy Juda.

Peacock (Sun Turkey) Kachina,
Tawa Koyung Kachina, 16" high.
(Colton #250, Wright page 152.)
Collection of Tom and Nancy Juda.

A set of *Heoto Mana* and Great Horned Owl Kachina, 14¾" high.

Heoto Mana. (Bassman page 16, Wright page 160.)

Great Horned Owl Kachina, *Mongwa*.
(Bassman page 17, Colton #78, Wright page 111.)
Collection of Tom and Nancy Juda.

Wildcat Kachina, *Tokoch*, 14¾" high.
(Colton #84, Wright page 31.)
Collection of Tom and Nancy Juda.

Left, Horse Kachina, *Kavai-i Kachina,* 16½"high.
(Bassman page 114, Colton #181, Wright page 139.)
Second Place at Gallup Inter-Tribal Indian Ceremonial in Gallup, New Mexico in 1987.
Collection of Theda and Michael Bassman.

Right, Long-haired Kachina, *Ang-ak-china,* 19" high.
(Bassman page 81, Colton #127, Wright page 172.)
Third Place at Gallup Inter-Tribal Indian Ceremonial in Gallup, New Mexico in 1986.
Private collection.

Flower Kachina, *Tsitoto,* 18" high.
(Colton #45, Wright page 30.)
Collection of Nick Smith.

Saviki, 19½" high.
(Colton #121, Wright page 96.)
Private collection.

Left, Cold-Bringing Woman or "Comb Hair Upwards" Maiden, *Horo Mana* or *Yohozro Wuhti,* 10¼" high.
(Bassman page 6, Colton #101, Wright page 34.)

Right, Mocking Kachina, *Kwikwilyaqa,* 9½" high.
(Bassman page 151, Colton #107, Wright page 37.)

Both Collection of Stiesmeyer family.

A set of a Red-bearded Long-haired Kachina and a Hano Long-haired Kachina Maiden, 15¾" high.

Red-bearded Long-haired Kachina, *Ang-ak-china.* (Bassman page 81, Colton #127, Wright page 172.)

Hano Long-haired Kachina Maiden, *Hano Man*a or *Hokyana Mana.* (Bassman page 109, Colton #191, Wright page 194.)

Private collection.

A set of a Kokopelli and Kokopelli Maiden, 6¾" high. Assassin or Robber Fly Kachina or Hump-backed Flute Player Kachina, *Kokopölö or Kokopelli.* (Bassman page 123, Colton #65, Wright page 109.)

Kokopelli Maiden, *Kokopölö Mana* or *Kokopelmana*. (Bassman page 123, Colton #66, Wright page 231.)

Collection of Tom and Nancy Juda.

"Man with Reeds Tied T
Söhönasomtaqa, 13¾" hig
(Colton #189, Wright page 62
Collection of Steve and Gloria Cowgi

Paralyzed Kachina, *Tühavi,* 11¾" high.
(Bassman page 107, Colton #144,
Wright page 123.)
Collection of Richard and Martha Burr.

Hano Mana, 12¾" high.
(Bassman page 109, Colton #264, Wright page 51.)
Private collection.

From left to right

Kachina Chief's Lieutenant, *Aholi,* 13" high. (Colton #8, Wright page 19.)

Skeleton Fetching Kachina, *Maswik Kachina* or *Masau'u Fetching Kachina,* 16¼". (Colton #115, Wright page 252.)

Kachina Maiden, *Hemis Kachin-mana* or *Kachin-mana,* 12½" high. (Bassman page 120, Colton #133, Wright page 215.)

All collection of Robert Broder.

Buffalo Dancer, *Mosairu*, 14" high.
(Bassman page 105.)
Collection of Tom and Nancy Juda.

Zuñi Fire God with Wolf,
Cholawitze, 13¾" high.
(Bassman page 25,
Colton #151,
Wright page 128.)
Private collection.

Buffalo Dancers, *Mosairu,* 14" high.
(Bassman page 105.)
First Place at Gallup Inter-Tribal Indian Ceremonial in Gallup, New Mexico in 1989.
Collection of Daniel and Christine Wolfus.

Left, Screech Owl Kachina, *Hotsko,* 15" high.
(Bassman page 15, Colton #80, Wright page 92.)
Collection of Tom and Nancy Juda.

Right, Corn Dance Leader, *Sotungtaka.* 15" high.
(Bassman page 31, Wright page 157.)
Collection of Michael and Carolyn McGuire.

Deer Kachina, *Sowí-ing Kachina*, 19" high.
(Bassman page 155, Colton #91, Wright page 166.)
Second Place at Gallup Inter-Tribal Indian Ceremonial in Gallup, New Mexico in 1989.
Collection of Theda and Michael Bassman.

Soyok Mana, 18" high.
(Bassman page 28, Colton #27, Wright page 77.)
Collection of Daniel and Christine Wolfus.

Chakwaina, 14¾" high.
(Bassman page 143, Colton #160, Wright page 99.)
Collection of Tom and Nancy Juda.

Ahote, *Ho-ó-te or Sakwahote*, 16" high.
(Bassman pages 20 and 21, Colton #104, Wright page 170.)
Second Prize at Gallup Inter-Tribal Indian Ceremonial in 1990.
Collection of Les and Pam Jensen.

Yesterday and Today

The following eighteen pages are illustrations of Cecil Calnimptewa's Kachina Doll carvings made in the mid 1970s and in 1979. Note the usage of actual feathers, fabrics, yarn, and bells. In contrast observe the same Kachina Dolls carved in 1982, the late 1980s, the early 1990s, up to the present day using wood only for all the appurtenances. These are remarkable examples in the evolution of his carving techniques and skills.

Yesterday, Kachina Chief, Eototo, 16" high. Made in mid-1970s. (Colton # 7, Wright page 18.) Collection of Nick Smith.

Today, Kachina Chief, *Eototo,* 15½" high. Made in 1992. (Colton #7, Wright page 18.) Collection of Tom and Nancy Juda.

Yesterday,
Kachina Chief's Lieutenant, *Aholi,* 19½".
Made in mid-1970s.
(Colton #8, Wright page 19.)
Collection of Nick Smith.

Today, Kachina Chief's Lieutenant, *Aholi,* 19" high. Made in 1991. (Colton #8, Wright page 19.) Collection of Theda and Michael Bassman.

Yesterday, Sun Kachina, *Tawa Kachina*, 16½" high.
Made in 1979. (Bassman page 110,
Colton #146, Wright page 124.)
Collection of G. M. Sollars.

Today, Sun Kachina, *Tawa Kachina,* 16½" high. Made in 1988. (Bassman page 110, Colton #146, Wright page 124.) Collection of Tom and Nancy Juda.

Yesterday, The Black Ogre's Uncle,
Tahaum Soyoko, 16" high.
Made in 1979.
(Colton #30, Wright page 79.)
Collection of G. M. Sollars.

Today, The Black Ogre's Uncle,
Tahaum Soyoko, 16" high.
Made in 1989.
(Colton #30, Wright page 79.)
Private collection.

Yesterday, Awatovi Ogre Woman, *Awatovi Soyok Wu-uti*, 14½" high.
Made in 1979. (Colton #25, Wright page 75.)
Collection of G. M. Sollars.

Today, Awatovi Ogre Man, *Awatovi Soyoktaqa,* 12¾" high.
Made in 1982. (Colton #26, Wright page 76.)
Collection of Louise and James Lawrence.

Yesterday, Crow Mother, *Angwusnasomtaqa* or *Tumas*, 18" high. Made in 1979. (Bassman page 99, Colton # 12, Wright page 66.) Collection of G. M. Sollars.

Today, Crow Mother, *Angwusnasomtaqa* or *Tumas,* 19" high. Made in 1991. (Bassman page 99, Colton #12, Wright page 66.) Collection of Tom and Nancy Juda.

Yesterday, *Mastof Kachina*, 15¼" high.
Made in 1979. (Bassman page 129, Colton #6, Wright page 13.)
Collection of G. M. Sollars.

Today, *Mastof Kachina*, 15" high.
Made in 1993. (Bassman page 129, Colton #6, Wright page 13.)
Collection of Theda and Michael Bassman.

Yesterday, The Germ God Kachina,
Mong Kachina or Chief Kachina, *Ahöla,* 15¾" high. Made in 1979.
(Bassman page 148, Colton #2, Wright page 9.)
Collection of G. M. Sollars.

Today, The Germ God Kachina,
Mong Kachina or Chief Kachina, *Ahöla,* 18½" high.
Made in 1994. (Bassman page 148,
Colton #2, Wright page 9.)
Collection of Theda and Michael Bassman.

Yesterday, Prickly Pear Cactus Kachina, *Yunya,* 15" high.
Made in 1979. (Colton #220, Wright page 146.)
Collection of G. M. Sollars.

Today, Prickly Pear Cactus Kachina, *Yunya,* 19" high. Made in 1994. (Colton #220, Wright page 146.) Private collection.

A set of an Eagle Kachina and a White Bear Kachina, 20" high.

Eagle Kachina, *Kwa Kachina*.
(Bassman page 22, Colton #71, Wright page 87.)

Bear Kachina, White, *Hon Kachina*.
(Bassman page 71, Colton #87, Wright page 114.)

Collection of Daniel and Christine Wolfus.

Chasing Star or Planet Kachina, *Na-ngasohu Kachina*, 17" high.
(Bassman page 111, Colton #148, Wright page 42.)
Collection of Tom and Nancy Juda.

Rio Grande Clown, *Tsuku,* 13" high.
(Colton #62, Wright page 242.)
Courtesy of McGee's Beyond Native Tradition.

Kachina Mother, *Hahai-i Wu-uti,* 9½" high.
This flat doll is called a Cradle Doll and is the first gift given to the newborn girl for her protection and to insure that she will take the correct path in becoming a responsible member of the Hopi tribe.
(Bassman page 129, Colton #44, Wright page 60.)
Collection of Les and Pam Jensen.

A set of a Black Ogre and a Rio Grande Clown, 15¼" high.

Black Ogre, *Nata-aska*.
(Bassman page 128, Colton #29,
Wright page 78.)

Rio Grande Clown, *Tsuku*.
(Colton #62, Wright page 242.)
Best of Division and First Place
at the Indian Market in
Santa Fe, New Mexico in 1988.

Collection of
Daniel and Christine Wolfus.

A Clown, *Kaisale,* 11" high.
(Bassman page 89, Colton #63,
Wright page 243.)
Private collection.

Red-tailed Hawk Kachina, *Palakwai,* 17" high.
(Bassman page 112, Colton #73, Wright page 61.)
Collection of Tom and Nancy Juda.

Kachina Priest, 9½" high. Private collection.

Left-handed Kachina with Dog, *Suy-ang-e-vif,* 11½" high.
(Bassman page 86, Colton #95, Wright page 32.)
Private collection.

A set of a Clown and The Mud Head Clown, 10¼" high.
Clown, *Hó-e or Wó-e* (Colton #40, Wright page 28.)
The Mud Head Clown, *Koyemsi.* (Bassman page 33, Colton #59, Wright page 238.)
Collection of Michael and Carolyn McGuire.

Butterfly Kachina Maiden,
Polik Mana or *Palhik Mana*, 7¼" high.
Entitled, "Taking a Break."
(Bassman page 93, Colton #120,
Wright page 106.)
Collection of Richard and Martha Burr.

Hano Clown or *Koshare, Paiyakyamu* or *Hano Chukuwai-upkia*, 14" high. (Bassman page 124, Colton #60, Wright page 239.) Collection of Tom and Nancy Juda.

Long-billed Kachina, *Wupomo Kachina,* 14½" high. (Colton #41, Wright page 29.)
First Place at the Indian Market in Santa Fe, New Mexico in 1991.
Private collection.

A set of an Eagle Kachina and a Mud Head Clown, 19½" high.
Eagle Kachina, *Kwa Kachina.* (Bassman page 22, Colton #71, Wright page 87.)
The Mud Head Clown, *Koyemsi.* (Bassman page 33, Colton #59, Wright page 238.)
Private collection.

Hilili, 17" high.
(Bassman page 143,
Colton #185, Wright page 43.)
Collection of Tom and Nancy Juda.

Left-handed Kachina,
Suy-ang-e-vif, 18" high.
(Bassman page 86,
Colton #95, Wright page 32.)
Best of Class, Best of Division,
and First Place at the Indian
Market in Santa Fe, New Mexico
in 1991. Private collection.

Left, Heheya's Uncle, *Heheya-aumutaqa*, 14¾" high. (Bassman page 19, Colton #36, Wright page 83.)
Right, *Heheya Kachin-mana*, 14½" high . (Bassman page 18, Colton #35, Wright page 82.)
Both collection of Tom and Nancy Juda.

Red-tailed Hawk Kachina,
Palakwai, 16¼" high.
(Bassman page 112,
Colton #73, Wright page 61.)
Private collection.

This set of the Snow Kachina Maiden, the Zuñi Kachina Maiden and the Kachina Maiden, is entitled, "Three Sisters," 14½" high.

Left, Snow Kachina Maiden, *Nuvak-chin-mana*. (Bassman page 96, Colton #100, Wright page 213) .

Middle, Zuñi Kachina Maiden, *Hoho Mana*. (Colton #156, Wright page 217).

Right, Kachina Maiden, *Hemis Kachin-mana* or *Kachin-mana*. (Bassman page 120, Colton #133, Wright page 215.) Best of Division and First Place at the Indian Market in Santa Fe, New Mexico in 1989.

Private collection.

Left-handed Kachina with Dog, *Suy-ang-e-vif,* 15" high.
(Bassman page 86, Colton #95, Wright page 32.)
Private collection.

The Deer Kachina Dance

Deer Kachina, *Sowí-ing Kachina,* (Bassman page 155, Colton #91, Wright page 166.)

From left to right.

17¼". Collection of Daniel and Christine Wolfus.
Second Place at the Indian Market in Santa Fe, New Mexico in 1989.

12". Collection of Tom and Nancy Juda.

16¼". Collection of Robert Broder.

19". Collection of Theda and Michael Bassman.
Second place at Gallup Inter-Tribal Indian Ceremonial in Gallup, New Mexico in 1989.

Turkey Kachina, *Koyona,* 12¾" high.
(Bassman pages 68 and 69, Colton #208, Wright page 104.)
Private collection.

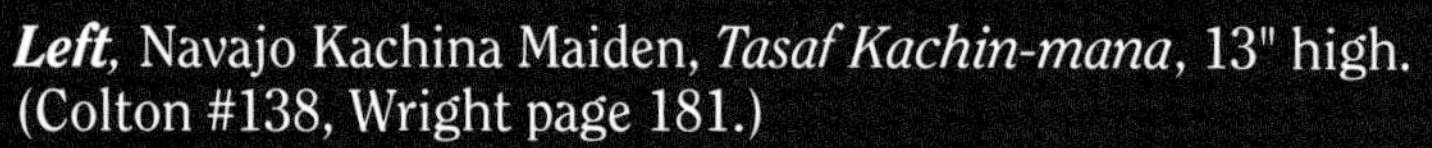

Left, Navajo Kachina Maiden, *Tasaf Kachin-mana*, 13" high.
(Colton #138, Wright page 181.)

Right, Navajo Kachina, *Tasaf Kachina,* A Navajo God Kachina (*Naastadji,* the Fringe Mouth God.) 16½" high.
(Colton #249, Wright page 151.)

Both from a private collection.

Warrior Maiden, *Hé-é-e,* 14¾" high.
(Bassman page 24, Colton #21, Wright page 57.)
Second Place at Gallup Inter-Tribal Indian Ceremonial in Gallup, New Mexico in 1987.

Collection of Theda and Michael Bassman.

Kachina Maiden, *Hemis Kachin-mana* or *Kachin-mana*, 15" high.
(Bassman page 120, Colton #133, Wright page 215.)
Private collection.

Kokopelli, Assassin or Robber Fly Kachina or Hump-backed Flute Player Kachina, *Kokopölö* or *Kokopelli,* 16¾" high. (Bassman page 123, Colton #65, Wright page 109.) Private collection.

Early Morning Kachina, *Talavai Kachina*, 11¼" high.
(Bassman page 13, Colton #108, Wright page 38.)
Collection of Robert Broder.

Blue Corn Maiden, *Sakwap Mana,* 14" high.
(Bassman page 102, Colton #165, Wright page 15.)
Private collection.

Basket Dancer, *Oaqol Mana*, 13" high.
Collection of Tom and Nancy Juda.

Eagle Kachina, *Kwa Kachina*, 11¾" high.
(Bassman page 22, Colton #71, Wright page 87.)
Collection of Louise and James Lawrence.

Sun Kachina, *Tawa Kachina,* 27" high
(Bassman page 110, Colton #146
Wright page 124.
Private collection

Horse Kachina, *Kavai-i Kachina,* 15" high.
(Bassman page 114, Colton # 181, Wright page 139.)
Collection of Tom and Nancy Juda.

Left, Cold-Bringing Woman or "Comb Hair Upwards" Maiden, *Horo Mana* or *Yohozro Wuhti,* 10¼" high.
(Bassman page 6, Colton #101, Wright page 34.)

Right, Snow Kachina Maiden, *Nuvak-chin-mana,* 15½" high.
(Bassman page 96, Colton #100, Wright page 213.)

Both collection of Robert Broder.

War Kachina Leader or Turquoise Nose Plug Man, *Kipok Kachina* or *Chospos-yaka-hentaka*, 17" high.
(Colton #140, Wright page 122.)
Collection of Tom and Nancy Juda.

Hano Mana, 14½" high.
(Bassman page 109, Colton #264, Wright page 51.)
Third Place at Gallup Inter-Tribal Indian Ceremonial in Gallup, New Mexico in 1989 .
Collection of Theda and Michael Bassman .

Crow Kachina, *Angwusi,* 17½" high.
(Bassman page 117, Wright page 158.)
Courtesy of Garland's Navajo Rugs.

Kachina Chief's Lieutenant, *Aholi*, 19" high.
(Colton #8, Wright page 19.)
Collection of Theda and
Michael Bassman.

Index, English Names

Index, Hopi Names